ICONS

BAMBOO STYLE

BAMBOO

Exteriors Interiors

STYLE

Details

PHOTOS **Reto Guntli**
EDITOR **Angelika Taschen**

TASCHEN

HONG KONG KÖLN LONDON LOS ANGELES MADRID PARIS TOKYO

Front cover: Courtyard views, home of C. C. Loo, Singapore.
Couverture: Fenêtres sur cour, chez C. C. Loo, Singapour.
Umschlagvorderseite: Innenhof-Impressionen auf dem Anwesen von C. C. Loo, Singapur.

Back cover: Natural spring water from a bamboo pipe, Yoshida Sanso, Kyoto, Japan.
Dos de couverture: Source naturelle jaillissant d'une canalisation en bambou, Yoshida Sanso, Kyoto, Japon.
Umschlagrückseite: Natürliches Quellwasser aus einem Bambusrohr bei Yoshida Sanso, Kyoto, Japan.

Also available from TASCHEN:

Inside Asia
2 volumes, 880 pages
ISBN: 978–3–8228–1441–3

To stay informed about upcoming TASCHEN titles, please request our magazine
at www.taschen.com/magazine or write to TASCHEN, Hohenzollernring 53, D-50672 Cologne,
Germany, contact@taschen.com, Fax: +49-221-254919. We will be happy to send you a free copy
of our magazine which is filled with information about all of our books.

Concept and editing by Angelika Taschen, Berlin
Layout and general project management by Stephanie Bischoff, Cologne
Texts by Daisann McLane, New York
Lithography by Horst Neuzner, Cologne
German Translation by Christiane Burkhardt/Norbert Pautner, Munich
French Translation by Manuel Benguigui for mot.tiff, Paris

Printed in Italy
ISBN: 978–3–8228–4967–5

CONTENTS SOMMAIRE INHALT

Let's begin with a riddle: What is stronger than steel, more beautiful than concrete, more flexible than wood, and far cheaper than glass or bricks? What can you eat for dinner, wear on your feet, play a melody with, and lounge upon? Bamboo is a magical plant, a material so versatile and useful that you have to remind yourself that it isn't a product of modern technology, but rather a common grass that grows wild in forests and gardens all over the world. "We cannot live without bamboo for a single day," wrote the Chinese poet Su Dungpo more than a thousand years ago. Back then, that was true – bamboo was essential, used for everything from transportation (rafts and boats) to housing. It was made into paper and medicine, and used in religious ceremonies. (The creation myth of the Philippines says that the first man and woman sprouted from a piece of bamboo.) As civilization progressed, and new building materials were discovered, bamboo's impor-

BAMBOO RISING
Daisann McLane

Une devinette pour commencer : qu'est-ce qui est plus résistant que l'acier, plus beau que le béton, plus souple que le bois et bien moins cher que le verre ou la brique ? Qu'est-ce que vous pouvez manger, porter aux pieds, utiliser pour jouer une mélodie ou pour vous étendre ? Le bambou est une plante magique, un matériau si polyvalent et si utile que c'est avec émerveillement que l'on se rappelle qu'il n'est pas issu de la technologie moderne, mais qu'il s'agit bel et bien d'une plante commune poussant dans les forêts et jardins du monde entier.« Nous ne saurions vivre un seul jour sans bambou », écrivait le poète chinois Su Dongpo il y a plus de mille ans. À cette époque, cette affirmation était à prendre au sens littéral : le bambou était essentiel. On l'utilisait pour tout, depuis le transport (par radeaux et bateaux) jusqu'à la construction des maisons. On en faisait du papier, des médicaments, et on l'utilisait au cours des cérémonies religieuses. (Dans le mythe de la création des Philippines, le premier homme et la première femme viennent d'un bambou.) Avec les progrès de la civilisation et la découverte de nouveaux matériaux de construction, le bambou a perdu de son importan-

Beginnen wir mit einem Rätsel: Was ist stabiler als Stahl, schöner als Beton, biegsamer als Holz und deutlich billiger als Glas oder Ziegel? Was lässt sich zum Abendessen zubereiten und an den Füßen tragen? Worauf kann man eine Melodie spielen und womit es sich gemütlich machen? Bambus ist ein magisches Material und so vielseitig und nützlich, dass man gern vergisst, dass es sich dabei um kein modernes Technologieprodukt, sondern um ein gemeines Gras handelt, das fast überall auf der Welt wildwachsend in Wäldern und Gärten anzutreffen ist. »Wir können nicht einen Tag ohne Bambus auskommen«, schrieb der chinesische Dichter Su Dungpo vor mehr als tausend Jahren. Damals war Bambus in der Tat überlebenswichtig und wurde für beinahe jeden Zweck verwendet – für Transportmittel (Flöße und Boote) ebenso wie für den Häuserbau. Man verarbeitete es zu Papier und Medizin und verwendete es für religiöse Zeremonien. (Nach dem Schöpfungsmythos der Philippinen sind Mann und Frau aus einem Stück Bambus entstanden.) Mit dem Fortschreiten der Zivilisation wurden neue Baumaterialien entdeckt und der Bambus verlor zunehmend an Bedeutung. Doch

tance declined. But now, as we head into a future of scarcer resources and limited energy, designers and architects worldwide are rediscovering bamboo's beautiful, natural qualities. Mankind has, for centuries, been drawn to the majesty of these soaring green stalks – Buddhist monks preferred meditating in bamboo groves, and the T'ang Dynasty poets met under the plant's whispering leaves, to get drunk and recite verse. The photographs in the following pages reveal how today's designers and architects weave bamboo's natural meditative magic into the contemporary built environment. From the elegant, formal verticals of bamboo in the sliding windows and slatted floors of the Kengo Kuma's modernist Bamboo Wall House near Beijing, to the breezy open platforms that erase the boundaries of "indoors" and "outdoors" in a house in Bali, bamboo surrounds us with ancient comfort, and modern soul.

ce. Cependant, alors que nous nous dirigeons vers un avenir où certaines ressources naturelles et énergétiques viendront à manquer, les designers et architectes du monde entier redécouvrent les vertus merveilleuses et naturelles du bambou. Depuis des siècles, l'humanité est fascinée par la majesté de ces grandes tiges vertes élancées : les moines bouddhistes aimaient à méditer dans des plantations de bambou et les poètes de la dynastie Tang se retrouvaient sous leurs feuilles bruissantes pour s'enivrer et déclamer leurs vers. Les photographies qui suivent révèlent la manière dont les designers et architectes d'aujourd'hui parviennent à introduire la magie naturelle du bambou dans un environnement contemporain. Depuis l'élégance formelle des panneaux de bambou utilisés pour les fenêtres coulissantes et les parquets de la moderne Maison aux Murs de Bambou, près de Pékin, jusqu'aux terrasses ouvertes aux vents des maisons balinaises, abolissant les frontières entre intérieur et extérieur, le bambou nous entoure, réconciliant confort à l'ancienne et modernité.

jetzt, wo die Ressourcen und Energievorräte knapp zu werden drohen, entdecken Designer und Architekten weltweit die wunderbaren Eigenschaften von Bambus aufs Neue. Der Mensch fühlt sich bereits seit Jahrhunderten von diesen majestätisch in die Höhe schießenden Stängeln angezogen. Buddhistische Mönche meditierten bevorzugt in Bambushainen. Auch die Dichter der Tang-Dynastie trafen sich unter raschelnden Bambusblättern, wo sie sich betranken und Verse rezitierten. Die Fotos auf den folgenden Seiten zeigen, wie heutige Designer und Architekten den natürlichen, meditativen Zauber von Bambus in ein zeitgenössisches bauliches Umfeld integrieren. Von den eleganten, strengen Bambussichtblenden und Lattenrostböden des modernistischen Bamboo Wall House unweit von Peking bis hin zu den luftigen, offenen Pfahlbauten auf Bali, bei denen die Grenzen zwischen Innen und Außen verschwimmen: Bambus sorgt für eine altvertraute Behaglichkeit und zeigt gleichzeitig sein modernes Gesicht.

"...Wintery wind
Becomes quiet
In the bamboo forest..."

Haiku by Basho, *Japanese poet*

«...Le vent d'hiver
s'apaise
dans la forêt de bambous...»

Haiku de Basho, *poète japonais*

»...Der Winterwind, ach ?
Verbarg sich im Bambushain
Und kam zur Ruhe...«

Haiku von Basho, *japanischer Dichter*

EXTERIORS

Extérieurs   Aussichten

10/11 Serenity: meditating in the Chizanso Garden, Zushi, Japan. *Sérénité dans le jardin Chizanso, Zushi, Japon.* Gelassenheit: Meditieren im Chinzanso-Garten, Zushi, Japan.

12/13 Fall flame: changing colors in bamboo garden, Shikoku, Japan. *Flamme d'automne : couleurs changeantes d'un jardin de bambous, Shikoku, Japon.* Herbstfeuer: Farbenspiel im Bambusgarten von Shikoku, Japan.

14/15 Andre Heller's bamboo garden in Gardone. *Le jardin de bambous d'André Heller à Gardone.* André Hellers Bambusgarten in Gardone.
Photo: Imagno/Franz Hubmann/Getty Images

16/17 Pond at Illuketia Villa, near Galle, Sri Lanka. *Étang de la villa Illuketia, près de Galle, Sri Lanka.* Teich der Illuketia Villa bei Galle, Sri Lanka.

18/19 Shaded comfort, Illuketia Villa, Sri Lanka. *Le confort de l'ombre, villa Illuketia, Sri Lanka.* Ein behaglicher Platz im Schatten, Illuketia Villa, Sri Lanka.

20/21 Traditional Thai cushion for relaxation at Vip's Villa, Chiang Mai. *Coussins thaïs traditionnels de relaxation à la villa Vip, Chiangmai.* In Vip's Villa von Chiang Mai lädt ein traditionelles Thai-Kissen zur Entspannung ein.

22/23 Bamboo shelters a cottage at Vip's Villa. *Le bambou abrite un pavillon à la villa Vip.* Bambus beschirmt eine Hütte in Vip's Villa.

24/25 Linda Garland's bamboo grove stilt house, Ubud, Bali. *La maison sur pilotis de Linda Garland au cœur d'une plantation de bambous, Ubud, Bali.* Linda Garlands Pfahlhaus in einem Bambushain von Ubud, Bali.

26/27 Natural haven: relaxing under thatched bamboo, Garland house, Ubud. *Un havre de paix naturel : relaxation sous un toit de bambou, maison de Linda Garland, Ubud.* Ein Naturparadies: Entspannung unter dem Bambusdach des Garland House in Ubud.

28/29 Secluded nook near Cynthia and John Hardy's house, Ubud, Bali. *Jardin secret, près de la maison de Cynthia et John Hardy, Ubud, Bali.* Ein einsames Plätzchen unweit des Hauses von Cynthia und John Hardy, Ubud, Bali.

30/31 Green haven, in Rolf and Helen von Bueren's house, Bangkok. *Havre de verdure, chez Rolf et Helen von Bueren, Bangkok.* Ein grüner Hafen in Rolf und Helen van Buerens Haus, Bangkok.

32/33 At the Tawaraya Ryokan, Kyoto, Japan. *Au Tawaraya Ryokan, Kyoto, Japon.* Im Tawaraya Ryokan in Kyoto, Japan.

34/35 Gateway to Tony and Margie Floirendo's house in Mindanao, Philippines. *Portail de la maison de Tony et Margie Floirendo à Mindanao, Philippines.* Eingangstor zum Haus von Tony und Margie Floirendo in Mindanao auf den Philippinen.

36/37 Bamboo bungalow at Barcelo Pearl Farm Island Resort, Philippines. *Bungalow de bambou au Barcelo Pearl Farm Island Resort, Philippines.* Bambusbungalow des Barcelo Pearl Farm Island Resort auf den Philippinen.

38/39 The temple of Ulun Danu, on Lake Bratan, Bali. *Temple Ulun Danu, sur le lac Bratan, Bali.* Der Tempel von Ulun Danu am Bratan-See auf Bali.
Photo: Michael K. Nichols/National Geographic/Getty Images

40/41 Fishermen on the Li River in Guilin, China. *Pêcheurs sur la rivière Li, à Guilin, Chine.* Fischer auf dem Li-Fluss in Guilin, China.
Photo: Dennis Cox/Time Life Pictures/Getty Images

42/43 Bamboo at the beach: the Floirendo house in Mindanao, Philippines. *Bambous sur la plage : la maison des Floirendo à Mindanao, Philippines.* Bambus am Strand: Das Haus der Floirendos in Mindanao auf den Philippinen.

44/45 Seaside deck at the Floirendo house in Mindanao. *Terrasse en bord de mer chez les Floirendo à Mindanao.* Terrasse mit Meerblick der Floirendos in Mindanao.

46/47 Traditional bamboo cottages at Barcelo Pearl Farm Island Resort. *Pavillons traditionnels en bambou au Barcelo Pearl Farm Island Resort.* Traditionelle Bambushütten des Barcelo Pearl Farm Island Resort.

48/49 Rustic shelter at Floirendo house, Mindanao, Philippines. *Cabane chez les Floirendo, Mindanao, Philippines.* Rustikaler Unterstand auf dem Anwesen der Floirendos in Mindanao, Philippinen.

50/51 Breakfast above the sea, at Barcelo Pearl Farm Island Resort. *Petit-déjeuner avec vue sur la mer, au Barcelo Pearl Farm Island Resort.* Frühstück mit Meerblick im Barcelo Pearl Farm Island Resort.

52/53 Minimalist elegance: the House of Bamboo in Kamakura, Japan. *Élégance minimaliste : la Maison du Bambou à Kamakura, Japon.* Minimalistische Eleganz: Das House of Bamboo in Kamakura, Japan.

54/55 Natural classic: at the Bamboo Wall house, near Beijing, China. *Classique naturel : la Maison aux Murs de Bambou, près de Pékin, Chine.* Natürliche Klassik: Das Bamboo Wall House unweit von Peking, China.

56/57 View of moveable bamboo partitions at Bamboo Wall House, Beijing. *Vue des cloisons mobiles de la Maison aux Murs de Bambou à Pékin.* Blick auf die Bambusschiebewände des Bamboo Wall House, unweit von Peking.

58/59 Bamboo windows filter light at Claska Hotel, Tokyo, Japan. *Les fenêtres en bambou filtrent la lumière à l'hôtel Claska, Tokyo, Japon.* Bambusfenster filtern das Licht im Claska Hotel, Tokyo, Japan.

60/61 Construction work: bamboo scaffolding at a Shanghai building site. *Échafaudages en bambou sur un chantier à Shanghai.* Bambusgerüst auf einer Baustelle in Shanghai. *Photo: Marie Mathelin/Roger Viollet/Getty Images*

62/63 Peasant woman selling bamboo baskets, Hanoi, Vietnam. *Paysanne vendant des paniers de bambou à Hanoi, Viêt-nam.* Eine Bäuerin verkauft Bambuskörbe, Hanoi, Vietnam. *Photo: Hoang Dinh Nam/AFP/Getty Images*

"…Meals can be without meat,
but living cannot be without bamboo…"
-
Su Dongpo, *Sung Dynasty Chinese poet*

«…On peut concevoir un repas sans viande,
mais on ne saurait vivre sans bambou…»
Su Dongpo, *poète chinois de la dynastie Sung*

»…Die Mahlzeit ohne Fleisch mag hingehen,
Doch kann ich ohne Bambus nicht bestehen…«
Su Dongpo, *chinesischer Dichter der Sung-Dynastie*

INTERIORS

Intérieurs   Einsichten

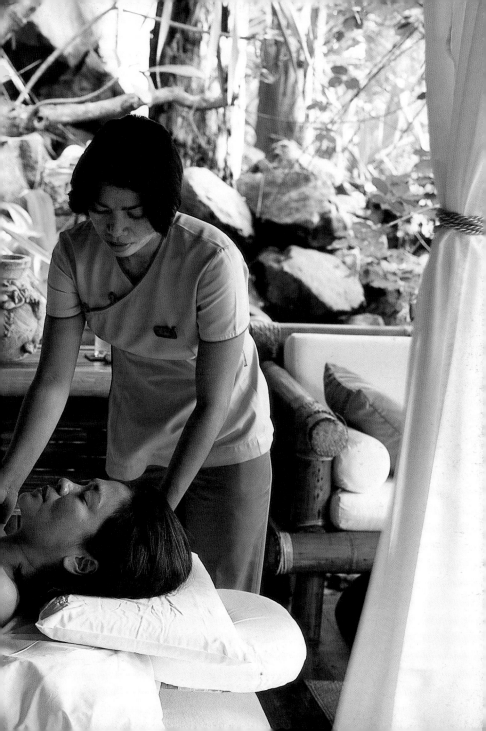

70/71 Bamboo curtain: at the Bamboo Wall House, near Beijing. *Rideau de bambou dans la Maison aux Murs de Bambou, près de Pékin.* Bambusvorhang im Bamboo Wall House, unweit von Peking.

72/73 Vertical drama: bamboo partitions at Bamboo Wall House. *Théâtre vertical : cloisons de bambou à la Maison aux Murs de Bambou.* Ein Lob der Vertikalen: Bambustrennwände im Bamboo Wall House.

74/75 Whispered elegance: dining room at Bamboo Wall House. *Élégance et chuchotements : salle à manger de la Maison aux Murs de Bambou.* Schlichte Eleganz: Esszimmer im Bamboo Wall House.

76/77 Shadows and light, at Bamboo Wall House, near Beijing. *Jeux d'ombre et de lumière à la Maison aux Murs de Bambou, près de Pékin.* Licht und Schatten im Bamboo Wall House, unweit von Peking.

78/79 Window to the sea: at House of Bamboo, Kamakura, Japan. *Fenêtre sur la mer à la Maison du Bambou, Kamakura, Japon.* Fenster mit Meerblick: Im House of Bamboo, Kamakura, Japan.

80/81 Tea ceremony, at House of Bamboo, Kamakura. *Heure du thé à la Maison du Bambou, Kamakura.* Teezeremonie im House of Bamboo, Kamakura.

82/83 Tatami room with bamboo screens, House of Bamboo. *Tatamis et stores de bambou, Maison du Bambou.* Tatami-Zimmer mit Bambus-Sichtblenden im House of Bamboo.

84/85 Bookshelves hidden behind bamboo screen, House of Bamboo. *Étagères dissimulées derrière des cloisons de bambou, Maison du Bambou.* Bücherregale hinter einer Bambus-Sichtblende.

86/87 Bamboo at Izumi San, one of Japan's few modernist houses. *Bambou à Izumi San, l'une des rares maisons japonaises de la période moderniste.* Bambus bei Izumi San, einem von Japans wenigen Häusern im Stil der Moderne.

88/89 Horizontal view: at House on Heeren Street, Melaka, Malaysia. *Vue horizontale : maison dans Heeren Street, Melaka, Malaisie.* Total horizontal: Das House on Heeren Street, Melaka, Malaysia.

90/91 Bamboo partitions at Sugimoto House, Kyoto, Japan. *Stores de bambou dans la maison Sugimoto, Kyoto, Japon.* Bambus-Trennelemente im Sugimoto House, Kyoto, Japan.

92/93 Shifting views at Sugimoto House, an 1870s Kyoto townhouse. *Vues changeantes dans la maison Sugimoto, construite dans les années 1870, à Kyoto.* Veränderliche Perspektiven im Sugimoto, einem Kyotoer Stadthaus aus den 1870er-Jahren.

94/95 Sliding bamboo doors, at Sugimoto House, Kyoto. *Portes coulissantes en bambou, maison Sugimoto, Kyoto.* Bambus-Schiebetüren im Sugimoto House, Kyoto.

96/97 Sunlight breaks through the mural cuts, at Rokkaku House, Kyoto, Japan. *Le soleil se glisse entre les ajours du mur dans la maison Rokkaku, Kyoto, Japon.* Sonne, die durch Maueröffnungen fällt, im Rokkaku House, Kyoto, Japan.

98/99 Bamboo comfort: furniture at Floirendo house, Philippines. *Confort du bambou : mobilier de la résidence des Floirendo, Philippines.* Behaglicher Bambus: Mobiliar im Haus der Floirendos auf den Philippinen.

100/101 Breezy and casual: sitting room at Sri's Garden House, Bangkok. *Simplicité et fraîcheur : salon de Sri's Garden House, Bangkok.* Luftig und lässig: Das Wohnzimmer im Sri's Garden House, Bangkok.

102/103 The bamboo roof at Inoue Fusaichiro's, Japan. *Le toit de bambou de la maison d'Inoué Fusaichiro, Japon.* Das Bambusdach von Inoue Fusaichiro, Japan.

104/105 The mid-century Minka House of Inoue Fusaichiro, Takasaki, Japan. *Maison d'Inoué Fusaichiro, datant du milieu du XXᵉ siècle, Takasaki, Japon.* Das in den 1950er-Jahren erbaute Minka-Haus von Inoue Fusaichiro, Takasaki, Japan.

106/107 Entry to Nathalie Saphon Ridel's house, Siem Reap, Cambodia. *Entrée de la maison de Nathalie Saphon Ridel, Siem Riep, Cambodge.* Eingangsbereich im Haus von Nathalie Saphon Ridel, Siem Reap, Kambodscha.

108/109 Nathalie Saphon Ridel and her son, Siem Reap. *Nathalie Saphon Ridel et son fils, à Siem Riep, Cambodge.* Nathalie Saphon Ridel mir ihrem Sohn, Siem Reap.

110/111 Bed with woven bamboo headboard, Barcelo Pearl Farm Island Resort, Philippines. *Tête de lit en bambou tressé, Barcelo Pearl Farm Island Resort, Philippines.* Bett mit geflochtenem Bambus-Kopfteil, Barcelo Pearl Farm Island Resort auf den Philippinen.

112/113 Bamboo dreams: canopy bed, Anneke's Guesthouse, Ubud, Bali. *Rêves de bambou : lit à baldaquin, maison d'hôtes d'Anneke, Ubud, Bali.* Bambusträume: Himmelbett in Anneke's Guesthouse, Ubud, Bali.

114/115 Bamboo wardrobes at Whale Island Resort, Vietnam. *Penderies en bambou au Whale Island Resort, Viêt-nam.* Bambusgarderoben im Whale Island Resort, Vietnam.

116/117 Spa treatment at Barcelo Pearl Farm Island Resort, Philippines. *Thalassothérapie au Barcelo Pearl Farm Island Resort, Philippines.* Spa-Behandlung im Barcelo Pearl Farm Island Resort auf den Philippinen.

"…In a hot season
I stay indoors.
No guest comes.
I unroll the bamboo blind
Sheltering my quiet room…"

Po Chu-I, *T'ang Dynasty Chinese poet*

«…À la saison chaude
Je reste à l'intérieur.
Nul ne vient me rendre visite.
Je déroule le volet de bambou
Pour préserver la tranquillité de ma chambre…»

Po Chu-I, *poète chinois de la dynastie Tang*

»…Zur heißen Jahreszeit bleib ich im Haus,
erwarte keinen Gast.
Der Bambusvorhang wird entrollt,
der meine stille Kammer schützt…«

Po Chu-I, *chinesischer Dichter der Tang-Dynastie*

DETAILS

Détails Details

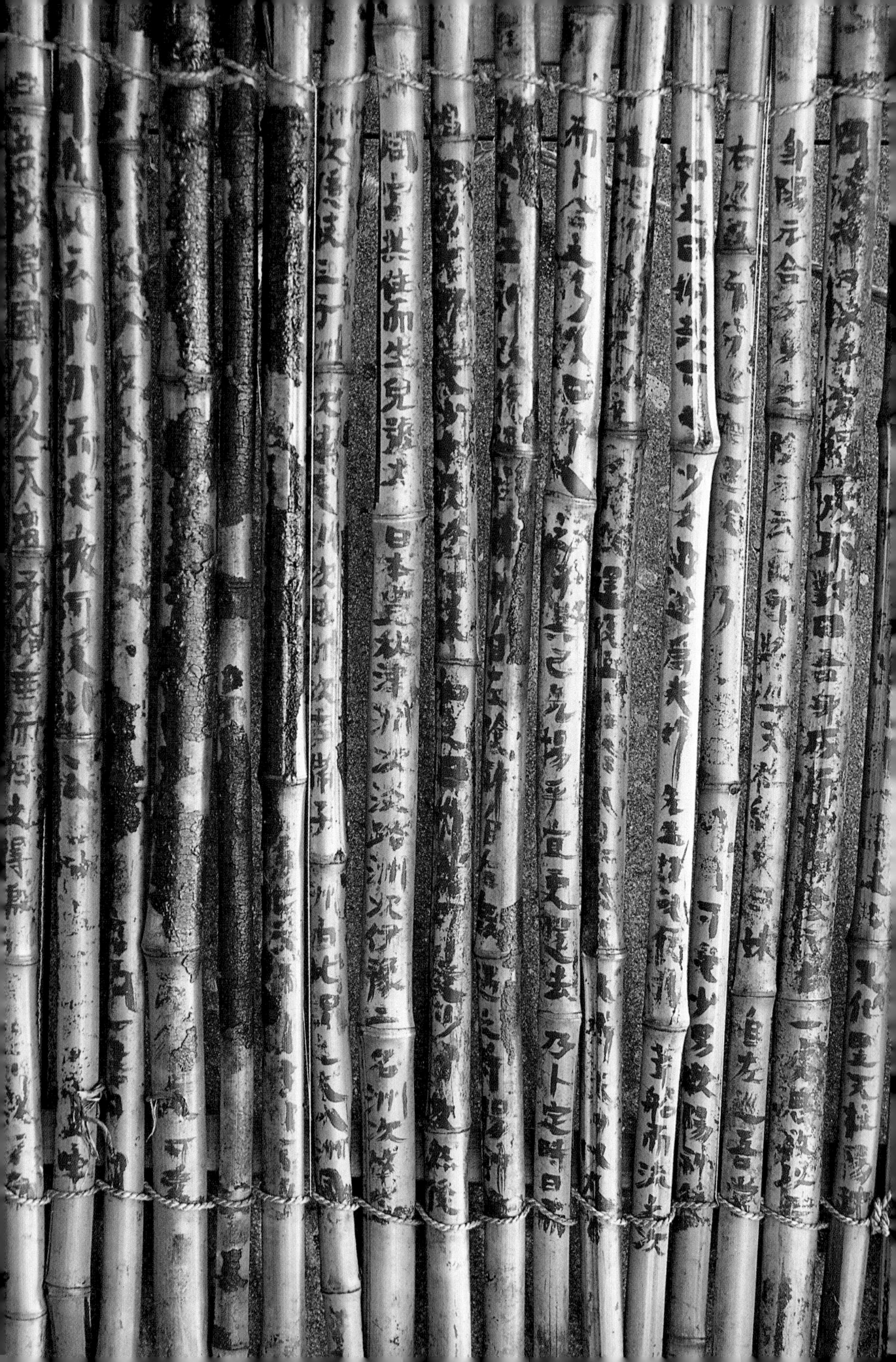

122 On the bamboo sheltered path, Hardy house, Ubud, Bali. *Sentier abrité par les bambous, chez les Hardy, Ubud, Bali.* Ein von Bambus gesäumter Weg beim Hardy House, Ubud, Bali.

124/125 Courtyard views, home of C.C. Loo, Singapore. *Fenêtres sur cour, chez C. C. Loo, Singapour.* Innenhof-Impressionen auf dem Anwesen von C. C. Loo, Singapur.

127 Outdoor shower at the House by the Reservoir, Singapore. *Douche extérieure dans la Maison du Réservoir, Singapour.* Freiluftdusche im Haus in der Nähe des Reservoirs, Singapur.

128 In the garden, Toni and Mari Escano's house, Manila, Philippines. *Dans le jardin de Toni et Mari Escano, Manille, Philippines.* Im Garten von Toni und Mari Escano, Manila, Philippinen.

129 Open bath with bamboo, at Carolina Tety's house, Bali. *Bain en plein air, sur fond de bambous, chez Carolina Tety à Bali.* Freiluftdusche mit Bambus auf dem Anwesen von Carolina Tety, Bali.

131 Bamboo-railed balcony, Taman Bebek Villas, Bali. *Balustrade en bambou, villas Taman Bebek, Bali.* Balkon mit Bambusgeländer, Taman Bebek Villas, Bali.

132 Naturally relaxed, at Garland house, Ubud, Bali. *Relaxation en pleine nature, chez Linda Garland, Ubud, Bali.* Entspannen inmitten der Natur im Garland House, Ubud, Bali.

133 Bamboo settee at Garland house, Ubud. *Canapé en bambou, chez Linda Garland, Ubud.* Bambus-Couch im Garland House, Ubud.

134 Shower au naturel, at Garland house in Ubud. *Douche au naturel, chez Linda Garland à Ubud.* Freiluftdusche im Garland House, Ubud.

136 An outdoor table at the House of Bamboo, Kamakura, Japan. *Table de jardin, Maison du Bambou, Kamakura, Japon.* Terrassentisch im House of Bamboo, Kamakura, Japan.

137 By the river at John Hardy's Shrimp House, Sayan, Bali. *Au bord de la rivière, Maison de la Crevette de John Hardy, Sayan, Bali.* Fluss-Steg des Shrimp House von John Hardy, Sayan, Bali.

138 Bamboo thicket at the Escano house in Manila. *Fourré de bambous, chez les Escano, Manille.* Bambusdickicht beim Escano House in Manila.

140 Green bamboo at House of Bamboo in Kamakura. *Bambou vert à la Maison du Bambou de Kamakura.* Grüner Bambus im House of Bamboo in Kamakura.

141 Freshly cut bamboo at Chinzanso Garden, Zushi, Japan. *Bambou fraîchement coupé au jardin Chinzanso, Zushi, Japon.* Frisch geschnittener Bambus im Garten von Chinzanso, Zushi, Japan.

143 Natural spring water from a bamboo pipe, Yoshida Sanso, Kyoto. *Source naturelle jaillissant d'une canalisation en bambou, Yoshida Sanso, Kyoto.* Natürliches Quellwasser aus einem Bambusrohr bei Yoshida Sanso, Kyoto.

144 Portal, with bamboo thicket beyond, Hardy house, Bali. *Porte avec bouquet de bambous en arrière-plan, résidence de John Hardy, Bali.* Tor mit Bambusdickicht im Hintergrund auf dem Hardy-House-Anwesen, Bali.

145 Spring water and bamboo cup, Sugimoto House, Kyoto, Japan. *Eau de source avec tasse en bambou, maison Sugimoto, Kyoto, Japon.* Quellwasser und Bambuskelle, Sugimoto House, Kyoto, Japan.

147 At Chiiori, a 300-year-old thatched farmhouse in Shikoku, Japan. *À Chiiori, une ferme vieille de 300 ans, Shikoku, Japon.* Chiiori, ein 300 Jahre altes Bauernhaus in Shikoku, Japan.

148 Bamboo footbridge at Hardy house, Ubud, Bali. *Passerelle en bambou, résidence de John Hardy, Ubud, Bali.* Bambusbrücke auf dem Anwesen des Hardy House, Ubud, Bali.

149 Round portal at Fusaichiro house, Takasaki, Japan. *Porte ronde chez Inoué Fusaichiro, Takasaki, Japon.* Mondtor im Fusaichiro House, Takasaki, Japan.

150 Bamboo garden, Eizo Shiina, Japan. *Jardin de bambous, Eizo Shiina, Japon.* Bambusgarten, Eizo Shiina, Japan.

152 Contrast in textures: bamboo wall at Sugimoto House. *Contraste des textures : mur de bambou dans la maison Sugimoto.* Kontrastreiche Bambuswand, Sugimoto House, Japan.

153 Bamboo and baby at Conchita Kien's "Villa Matisse" in Bali. *Bambou et bébé dans la villa Matisse de Conchita Kien à Bali.* Bambus und Baby in Conchita Kiens »Villa Matisse« auf Bali.

154 Sandy serenity: at the House of Bamboo, Kamakura, Japan. *Sérénité du sable à la Maison du Bambou, Kamakura, Japon.* Sandfarbene Heiterkeit: House of Bamboo, Kamakura, Japan.

156 Stilt cottages at Barcelo Pearl Farm Island Resort, Philippines. *Pavillons sur pilotis au Barcelo Pearl Farm Island Resort, Philippines.* Pfahlbauten des Barcelo Pearl Farm Island Resort auf den Philippinen.

157 Bamboo screen at Izumi San, Japan. *Rideau de bambou à Izumi San, Japon.* Bambus-Sichtblende, Izumi San, Japan.

158 High bamboo roof shelters a sitting area, Villa Samadhana, Bali. *Salon abrité par un haut toit en bambou, villa Samadhana, Bali.* Wohnlandschaft in hoher Bambushütte, Villa Samadhana, Bali.

160 Woven bamboo wall, Batangas Province, Philippines. *Mur tressé en bambou, province de Batangas, Philippines.* Geflochtene Bambuswand, Provinz-Batangas, Philippinen.

161 Bamboo faucet at House of Bamboo, Kamakura, Japan. *Robinet en bambou, Maison du Bambou, Kamakura, Japon.* Bambuswasserhahn im House of Bamboo, Kamakura, Japan.

162 Exterior of Cala Perdida in Batangas Province, Philippines. *Vue de la Cala Perdida, province de Batangas, Philippines.* Fassade, Cala Perdida in der Provinz Batangas, Philippinen.

164 Woven bamboo walls in Furniture House, near Beijing, China. *Murs tressés en bambou, Maison du Mobilier, Pékin, Chine.* Geflochtene Bambuswände im Furniture House, unweit von Peking, China.

165 Dining area at the Furniture House, near Beijing. *Salle à manger, Maison du Mobilier, près de Pékin.* Esszimmer im Furniture House, unweit von Peking.

167 Bamboo screens and calligraphy decorate Tokyo's Nihon Miyabigoto Club. *Calligraphies et panneaux de bambou décorent le Nihon Miyabigoto Club de Tokyo.* Bambus-Stellwände und Kalligraphien schmücken Tokyos Nihon Miyabigoto Club.

168 Bamboo calligraphy brushes, Nihon Miyabigoto Club. *Matériel de calligraphie en bambou, Nihon Miyabigoto Club.* Kalligraphie-Pinsel aus Bambus im Nihon Miyabigoto Club.

169 Slatted sunlight falls on modular sofa, Bamboo Wall House, China. *Rais de lumière tombant sur un sofa modulaire, Maison aux Murs de Bambou, Chine.* Sonne fällt durch eine Bambusblende auf ein Sofa, Bamboo Wall House, China.

170 Detail, House of Bamboo, Kamakura, Japan. *Détail, Maison du Bambou, Kamakura, Japon.* Detail im House of Bamboo, Kamakura, Japan.

172 A corner at the Nihon Miyabigoto Club, Tokyo. *Recoin du Nihon Miyabigoto Club, Tokyo.* Ecke im Nihon Miyabigoto Club, Tokyo.

173 Surrounded by bamboo, Bamboo Wall House, China. *Du bambou partout, Maison aux Murs de Bambou, Chine.* Bambus, wohin man schaut: Bamboo Wall House, China.

175 Bamboo sculpture over fireplace, House of Bamboo, Japan. *Sculpture en bambou au-dessus de la cheminée, Maison du Bambou, Japon.* Bambus-Skulptur über dem Kamin, House of Bamboo, Japan.

176 Detail of bamboo sculpture, House of Bamboo. *Détail de la sculpture en bambou, Maison du Bambou.* Detail der Bambus-Skulptur, House of Bamboo.

177 Staircase at the House of Bamboo. *L'escalier de la Maison du Bambou.* Treppe im House of Bamboo.

178 Passageway at Tawaraya Ryokan, Kyoto, Japan. *Galerie de Tawaraya Ryokan, Kyoto, Japon.* Durchgang im Tawaraya Ryokan, Kyoto, Japan.

180 Bamboo lattice at Iori foundation house, Oshikoji, Japan. *Treillis en bambou à la Fondation Iori, Oshikoji, Japon.* Bambusgitter im Iori Foundation House, Oshikoji, Japan.

181 Detail, Alex Kerr's Tenmangu house, near Kyoto. *Détail de la maison Tenmangu d'Alex Kerr, près de Kyoto.* Detail in Alex Kerrs Tenmangu House, unweit von Kyoto.

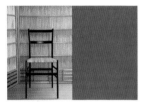   

182 A corner in the Yagi House, Osaka, Japan. *Recoin de la maison Yagi, Osaka, Japon.* Eine Ecke im Yagi House, Osaka, Japan.

184 Bamboo paper fans at Chiiori farmhouse, Shikoku, Japan. *Éventails en papier de bambou à la ferme Chiiori, Shikoku, Japon.* Bambuspapierfächer im Chiiori-Bauernhaus, Shikoku, Japan.

185 Antique kimono on bamboo hangar, Sugimoto House, Japan. *Kimono ancien dans une cabane en bambou, maison Sugimoto, Japon.* Antiker Kimono auf einem Bambus-Kleiderständer, Sugimoto House, Japan.

187 A bamboo serving tray at House of Bamboo, Japan. *Plateau de service en bambou, Maison du Bambou, Japon.* Bambus-Tablett aus dem House of Bamboo, Japan.

**The Hotel Book. Great Escapes
South America** Christiane
Reiter / Ed. Angelika Taschen /
Hardcover, 360 pp. / € 29.99/
$ 39.99 / £ 24.99 / ¥ 5.900

**The Hotel Book. Great Escapes
North America** Daisann
McLane / Ed. Angelika Taschen /
Hardcover, 400 pp. / € 29.99/
$ 39.99 / £ 24.99 / ¥ 5.900

**The Hotel Book. Great Escapes
Asia** Christiane Reiter /
Ed. Angelika Taschen / Hardcover,
400 pp. / € 29.99 / $ 39.99 /
£ 24.99 / ¥ 5.900

"This is one for the coffee table, providing more
than enough material for a good drool. Gorgeousness
between the cover." —*Time Out*, London, on *Great Escapes Africa*

"Buy them all and add some pleasure to your life."

60s Fashion
Ed. Jim Heimann

70s Fashion
Ed. Jim Heimann

African Style
Ed. Angelika Taschen

Alchemy & Mysticism
Alexander Roob

American Indian
Dr. Sonja Schierle

Angels
Gilles Néret

Architecture Now!
Ed. Philip Jodidio

Art Now
Eds. Burkhard Riemschneider,
Uta Grosenick

Atget's Paris
Ed. Hans Christian Adam

Bamboo Style
Ed. Angelika Taschen

Ingrid Bergman
Ed. Paul Duncan, Scott Eyman

Berlin Style
Ed. Angelika Taschen

Humphrey Bogart
Ed. Paul Duncan, James Ursini

Marlon Brando
Ed. Paul Duncan,
F.X. Feeney

Brussels Style
Ed. Angelika Taschen

Cars of the 50s
Ed. Jim Heimann,
Tony Thacker

Cars of the 60s
Ed. Jim Heimann, Tony Thacker

Cars of the 70s
Ed. Jim Heimann, Tony Thacker

Charlie Chaplin
Ed. Paul Duncan, David Robinson

China Style
Ed. Angelika Taschen

Christmas
Ed. Jim Heimann, Steven Heller

Design Handbook
Charlotte & Peter Fiell

Design for the 21st Century
Eds. Charlotte & Peter Fiell

Design of the 20th Century
Eds. Charlotte & Peter Fiell

Marlene Dietrich
Ed. Paul Duncan,
James Ursini

Devils
Gilles Néret

Robert Doisneau
Ed. Jean-Claude Gautrand

East German Design
Ralf Ulrich/Photos: Ernst Hedler

Clint Eastwood
Ed. Paul Duncan, Douglas
Keesey

Egypt Style
Ed. Angelika Taschen

Encyclopaedia Anatomica
Ed. Museo La Specola Florence

M.C. Escher

Fashion
Ed. The Kyoto Costume Institute

Fashion Now!
Eds. Terry Jones, Susie Rushton

Fruit
Ed. George Brookshaw,
Uta Pellgrü-Gagel

HR Giger
HR Giger

Grand Tour
Harry Seidler

Cary Grant
Ed. Paul Duncan, F.X. Feeney

Graphic Design
Eds. Charlotte & Peter Fiell

Greece Style
Ed. Angelika Taschen

Halloween
Ed. Jim Heimann,
Steven Heller

Havana Style
Ed. Angelika Taschen

Audrey Hepburn
Ed. Paul Duncan, F.X. Feeney

Katharine Hepburn
Ed. Paul Duncan, Alain Silver

Homo Art
Gilles Néret

Hot Rods
Ed. Coco Shinomiya, Tony
Thacker

Hula
Ed. Jim Heimann

India Bazaar
Samantha Harrison, Bari Kumar

London Style
Ed. Angelika Taschen

Steve McQueen
Ed. Paul Duncan, Alain Silver

Mexico Style
Ed. Angelika Taschen

Miami Style
Ed. Angelika Taschen

Minimal Style
Ed. Angelika Taschen

Marilyn Monroe
Ed. Paul Duncan,
F.X. Feeney

Morocco Style
Ed. Angelika Taschen

New York Style
Ed. Angelika Taschen

Paris Style
Ed. Angelika Taschen

Penguin
Frans Lanting

20th Century Photography
Museum Ludwig Cologne

Pierre et Gilles
Eric Troncy

Provence Style
Ed. Angelika Taschen

Robots & Spaceships
Ed. Teruhisa Kitahara

Safari Style
Ed. Angelika Taschen

Seaside Style
Ed. Angelika Taschen

Signs
Ed. Julius Wiedeman

South African Style
Ed. Angelika Taschen

Starck
Philippe Starck

Surfing
Ed. Jim Heimann

Sweden Style
Ed. Angelika Taschen

Tattoos
Ed. Henk Schiffmacher

Tiffany
Jacob Baal-Teshuva

Tokyo Style
Ed. Angelika Taschen

Tuscany Style
Ed. Angelika Taschen

Valentines
Ed. Jim Heimann,
Steven Heller

Web Design: Best Studios
Ed. Julius Wiedemann

Web Design: Best Studios 2
Ed. Julius Wiedemann

Web Design: E-Commerce
Ed. Julius Wiedemann

Web Design: Flash Sites
Ed. Julius Wiedemann

Web Design: Music Sites
Ed. Julius Wiedemann

Web Design: Portfolios
Ed. Julius Wiedemann

Orson Welles
Ed. Paul Duncan,
F.X. Feeney

Women Artists
in the 20th and 21st Century
Ed. Uta Grosenick

ICONS